TRENDY RESTAURANTS IN CHINA
2004 © PAGE ONE PUBLISHING PRIVATE LIMITED

First published in 2004 by
Page One Publishing Private Limited
20 Kaki Bukit View
Kaki Bukit Techpark II
Singapore 415956
Tel: (65) 6742-2088
Fax: (65) 6744-2088
enquiries@pageonegroup.com
www.pageonegroup.com

Distributed by:
Page One Publishing Private Limited
20 Kakit Bukit View
Kaki Bukit Techpark II
Singapore 415956
Tel: (65) 6742-2088
Fax: (65) 6744-2088

Printed by: LeeFung-Asco Printers Holdings Limited
Chief Editor: Chen Ci Liang
Cover Design: Kelley Cheng   Meng Xinxin
Format Design: Kelley Cheng   Meng Xinxin
Senior Editor: Zhang Shu Hong
Examiner: Dong Ge

ISBN: 981-245-113-7

All rights reserved. No part of this book may be used or reproduced in any manner whatsoever without written permission except in the case of brief quotations embodied in critical articles and reviews. For information, address Page One Publishing Private Limited, 20 Kaki Bukit View, Kaki Bukit Techpark II, Singapore 415956

Printed in China

TRENDY RESTAURANTS IN CHINA

HONG KONG · MALAYSIA · SINGAPORE · TAIWAN · THAILAND

CONTENTS

p.4 yè shanghai

p.20 people 6

p.36 crystal jade restaurant

p.52 the door restaurant & bar

p.76 shanghai tmsk restaurant

p.86 level 1 multi-cuisine restaurant

p.96 shark's fin & rice restaurant

p.108 soahc restaurant & tea garden

p.120 shintori null II

p.134 zen

p.146 park 97

p.160 san qian yuan sqy

p.174 banker cafe

p.182 shanghai uncle restaurant

p.196 liu hui guan restaurant

p.206 lipis lazuli international

p.212 mei long zhen restaurant

p.230 si fang cai restaurant

p.242 hei san yu zhuang

p.252 a-money restaurant

p.262 xintiandi shanghai

PREFACE

China is fast becoming an economic power, but prior to this, it has always been a centre of gastronomic delights. Trade, terrain, weather, customs, cultures and traditions have built a multitude of culinary tastes and dining styles. China's major cities function as the melting pot of Oriental and Western cultures today. While in the past, the design of restaurants may parallel certain styles in fashion, there is an increasing imperative for a restaurant's design to reflect the intricacies of its particular cuisine, with sprinklings of architectural and visual reminders from its cultural roots.

The interiors featured here are a harmonisation of the traditional and the modern, with the exploration of contemporary design concepts. *Trendy Restaurants in China* showcases a wide spectrum of contemporary projects—each with its unique application of decors and colors that pay tribute to its rich and colorful origins.

yè shanghai

Yè Shanghai is located in an old, classical building along an old lane at Xintiandi in Shanghai. With a contemporary charm injected into the building that was built in 1928, Yè Shanghai is an elegant blend of both the traditional and the contemporary. Adopting elements from both the past as well as the present, spacing the designer has given the spatial layout a new contemporary feel, while retaining the dark timber tones of the original building on the floor, architraves, roof and eaves in order to retain the essence of the past. Divided spatially into a relatively more private upper dining space—segmented into rooms which can be converted into a larger function room when required—and a lower main dining area, the restaurant takes on an innovative yet functional approach in the layout of a traditional *Shikumen*.

The entrance into the restaurant is a procession through a transitional gallery space where a waiting lounge is located. With its clean, modern lines and European inspired furniture, the space is stylish and dignified. For feasts and grand banquets, guests are able to choose the grand Chater Room located on the upper level. The luxurious space with a high ceiling and exposed roof rafters provides a unique experience for the guests at Yè Shanghai. The other four rooms on the upper level comprise of a mini function room with eight tables, an open area with a neat composition of U-shaped booths and dining tables for two, and two other smaller private dining rooms. Each of these rooms is designed differently, and each of them is adorned with authentic paintings and sculptures. The lower level comprises of private Retro-style booths and private dining tables. The feel of Yè Shanghai is fusion of both the East and the West, the old and the new, seamlessly intertwined in the design of this exquisite restaurant.

1. The dramatic play of lights give a luxurious feel to the space.
2. Glass doors visually connect the inside and the outside, while the black wooden doors are for privacy of the guests.

3. The design of the traditional Shikumen is transformed
4. The design retains the traditional spatial features of the Shikumen
5. One of the private rooms on the upper level
6. The glass railing acts as a barricade as well as a visual connection between the two sections of the upper dining area
7. The neatly arranged open dining area on the upper level
8. The translucent fabric shields and reveals at the same time

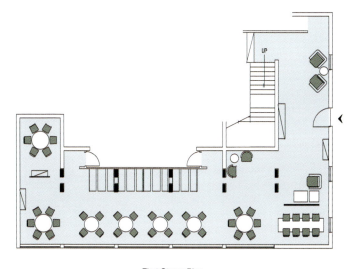

First Storey Plan

9. The original beams and rafters are retained to maintain the essence of the original structure
10. The contrast between dark and light shades give a dramatic and elegant feel to the space

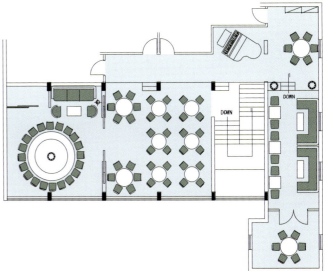

Second Storey Plan

11. The open casual dining area on the lower level
12. Silk fabrics are used as partitions to divide the space functionally

13. The use of color on the lampshade gives an Oriental feel to the lower lounge area
14. Plants and flowers accent the space with warmth and color
15. The lounge area on the lower level of the restaurant
16. One of the private rooms at Yé Shanghai
17. The long table in one of the private rooms on the lower level
18. The black screen against the contrast of the red fabric give a dignified air to the lounge area
19. A western-style private dining room on the lower level

20. The blend of the east and the west at the piano lounge on the upper level
21. The linear stairway that leads guests to the upper level
22. The full-height mirror is used to accentuate the height of the ceiling
23. Retro-style booths set against bamboo blinds on the lower level

22

23

24. The courtyard of the Shikumen is covered with a glass roof, transforming it into a modern dining area
25. Deep red is used throughout, giving it a rich and intense atmosphere
26. The design of the cellar is a blend of the east and the west
27. Clean modern lines and European furniture give a sense of class to the lounge area
28. The linear and geometrical arrangement of the restaurant give visual continuity to the space
29. The lounge area of the restaurant

people 6
people 6

On Yue Yang Road, with luxuriant phoenix trees on either side, sits People 6 – a new concept Shanghai restaurant incorporating broad and diverse styles. Unlike the common Chinese restaurant, People 6 combines the eastern Zen-conception with a simple industrial style to make a contemporary dining place. The design theme of the restaurant follows the prose: "Bamboo wet by rain, bridge of cloud overhangs, pavilion accompanies the moon, and a reality of dreams." The entrance of People 6 is designed with steel screens punctured by holes. Without question, this unique design can draw much attention from passers-by in the metropolis. After an introduction of bamboo, comes the interior of the restaurant. The beams and columns make the restaurant feel more likel a bare structural sculpture than a typical restaurant. The glass stairs, wall and balustrade, and the whole suspending dinning area, all together project a stunning and contemplative atmosphere. Bare steel elements, such as the bar, also accentuate the visual effect. The lighting seems quite mysterious and is at times surprising. An open and simple design style is the main characteristic of the third floor. Indirect lighting projects a sense of mysticism and simplicity. It would be more appropriate to say that the environment of People 6 is more "Zen" than cool and modern.

1. The design of the main gate is created by 36 holes that are bored through heavy-duty stainless steel plates
2. Exposed beams and bolts give a modern, industrial touch to the space
3. The superimposition of the hard metals against a minimal landscape setting makes an inviting entrance
4. The bamboo-lined entrance is inspired by poetry
5. Tables arranged on an elevated platform give a simulated feeling of lightness and suspension
6. The main entrance of People 6
7. The transparent lift shaft dynamically connects the different levels of the restaurant.

8. The play of strong beams of light highlights the dining tables and adds to the visual interest and overall geometry of the space
9. Light is used to create the effect of night
10. Strong geometry is balanced with the expanse of space and texture in this restaurant
11. The complete openness and spaciously laid-out seating arrangements gives a feeling of indirect privacy
12. The exposed beams visually compartmentalize the space as well as shields the lower levels from direct view.
13. Concrete floor and white dining chairs give an air of simplicity and a contemporary edge to the restaurant
14. Reflections and light add to the drama of the place

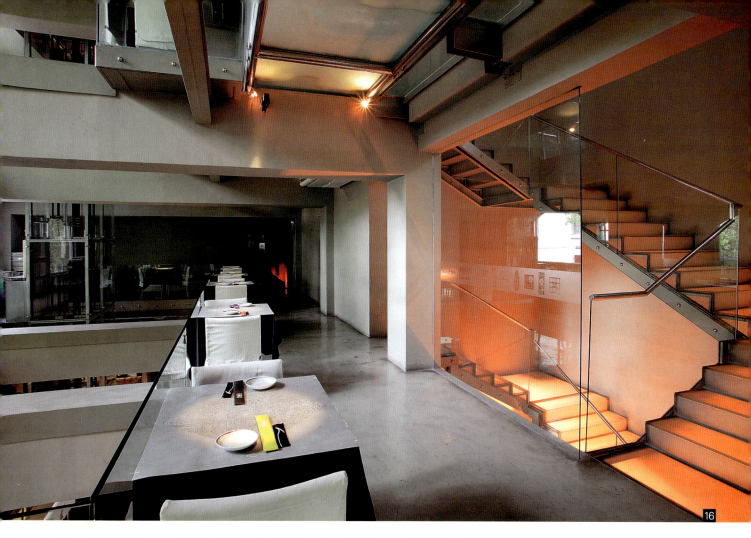

15. The glass railing serves as a safety feature as well as provides visual connections between the different levels
16. The logo is repeated throughout the restaurant
17. Light is shone through the glass staircase, thus giving it a suspended effect
18. Large picture windows allow the trees from the outside to act as backdrops
19. The windows provide a feeling of spaciousness and bring the landscape into the interior of the lounge area at the same time
20. Seating for two or four is composed in a linear fashion

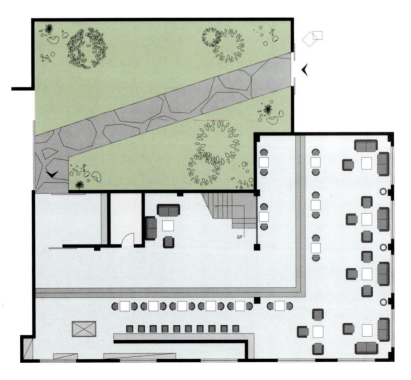

First Storey Plan

21. Partitions are used for privacy as well as spatially divide one section from the other
22. The combination of steel and glass are the key features on the third floor
23. The contrast of white and dark navy accentuate the spaciousness of the restaurant
24. The arch-shaped steel handrail softens the strong geometrical lines, and provides movement to the restaurant

crystal jade restaurant

restaurant

The Crystal Jade Restaurant, located along the south lane of Xintiandi, gives a strong visual impact with its play of lines and textures. The entrance passageway is lined with bricks, which is suggestive of the traditional Chinese forecourt and pavements. The narrow curvilinear corridor follows the form of the original structure. Repetitive timber members subtly shield and divide one space from the other. The use of mirrors on the ceiling gives an illusion of space and continuity. The expanse of space, visually and spatially interrupted by red light shafts, provides an extravagant visual feast. Swirling motions and colors, reflected from the huge mirrored ceiling, bring life to the restaurant. The rear of the restaurant is composed of a long table that stretches endlessly along the width. Besides the employment of red, subtle motifs and accents (like the lanterns used), give an opulent Oriental feel to the restaurant.

1. The rear of the restaurant with the long table
2. Full-height light shafts accentuate the height of the space
3. The palette of simple lines and strong colors
4. Lanterns give an Oriental touch to the space
5. The white dinnerware serves as accents to the deep tones of the furniture

6. The swirling superimposition of lines and textures gives a lively yet dizzying effect
7. Round tables are used for traditional communal dining
8. Red light pillars are used repetitively throughout
9. The lighting plays an important role in the creation of the space
10. Glass pillars serve to both expand the space and create an emotional effect
11. The visual effect at the entrance

12. Longitudinally-arranged chairs bear notable design in their backs, which form a new surface
13. The cross arrangement of the seats considers function and character
14. An expansive mirrored ceiling reflects the action which brings a room to life
15. The corridor is at once open and reserved
16. The impressive design incorporates clever lighting into the layout
17. The irregularly shaped dining area near the entry creates a unique feel

15

16

18

19

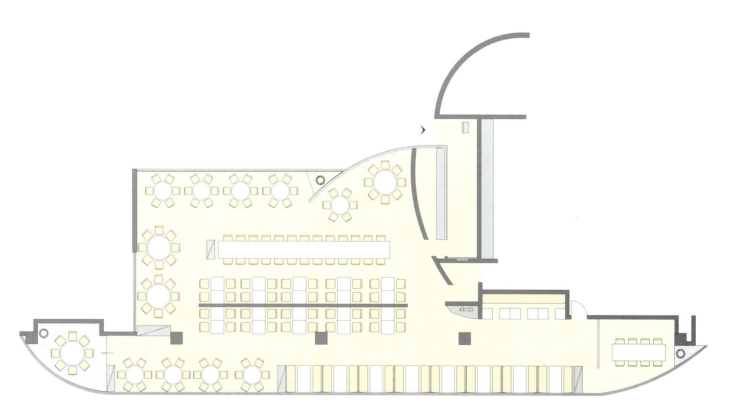

Floor Plan

18. Inverse lamps expresses a modern style
19. The mottled background of Chinese ink not only offers a surprise, but also brings a Zan feel
20. Repeated incisions across the space create a highly articulated surface. Where the eyes rest is up to the individual
21. The skillful use of red stripes re-interprets the simplicity of the dining chairs
22-23. The extravagant dining chair design endows the space with a rich aesthetic

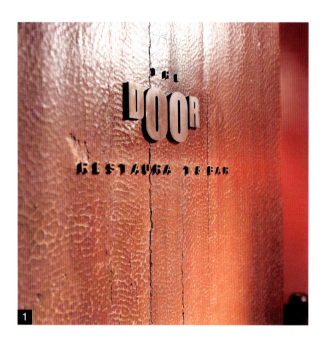

the door restaurant & bar

The Door Restaurant & Bar is immersed in an English castle-style setting. Its design concept combines charming modern elements with a classic antique style, creating an East-meets-West theme. The establishment adopts classic Chinese elements to set up a new conception and a new vision. Though the main business of the restaurant is Western food, traditional square Chinese timber tables are used. The style of restaurant and bar is elegant, showing both mysticism and nobleness. Past and present are separated by such features as the stone torii, Spanish wall pictures, shoji lamps, the handrail carved with a vivid dragon motif, and a large bell, which was made in the Qing Dynasty. All these elements constitute a grand and elegant environment, in which Chinese elements are dominant. The most significant features of The Door are its doors. There are about 40 doors in the restaurant, and all of them are genuine articles, such as the elegant carved *Kuihua* door, the grand *Yamen* door, and the simple family-style door. A carved bluestone-archway stands at one side of the lobby, vividly contrasting with the modern automatic door. As one ascends the timber stairs to the third floor, an old red timber door appears. What lies behind the red door is surprising; there is a stone figure of Buddha, which is combined with an eastern Zen-style setting in one corner of the restaurant. Each area adds to the overall effect which is sought—a unique and comfortable environment. An effect of smooth spatial transition has been created through the application of various kinds of display items, for example, joss sticks, candleholders, antique clocks, bird cages and panels carved with flowers. The overall scheme shows that the designer has a great interest in traditional Chinese culture and Buddhist art. He should not only be considered to be an enthusiastic antique collector, but also a trend-setter.

1. The name "DOOR" came from the book of "CHANGE". It means "the life cycle will continue forever"
2. Elaborate chandeliers drip elegance over the restaurant
3. Classic Chinese furniture has a stately feel
4. In order to fit into its surroundings (in JiangXi province), crude structural materials were chose
5. An attic both enriches the spatial hierarchy and increases the business area
6. A glance at the lobby
7. A significant feeling in this restaurant is "silence", which requires delicate observation

8. The figure of Buddha is a favourite of the designer
9. The design theme of the restaurant is based on a collection of 38 doors from various places and various times
10. The carved bluestone archway stands in the most striking location of the restaurant

11. The suspended ceiling is unique. It induces curiosity in the visitor, and forms an unexpected decorative focal point

12. The architecture is quite precise and formal

13. In order to reach a perfect design style, sacrifices were made to the business needs. For instance, a row of columns; a larger bar. These sacrifices made the restaurant more cosy and unique

14. In one corner of the bar, the figure of Buddha pervades

15. Soft chiffon separates a relatively private space.

16. Though the main business of the restaurant is Western food, traditional square Chinese timber tables are used

17. Door's bar is tidy
18. All the décor is historic; that's why the environment has an old-time feel
19. Comfortable leather seats in the drinking area
20. The Chinese wall mural is by a Spanish artist
21. The corridor to the private VIP room. It is big enough for a pint-sized banquet
22. The blocky form of the gate, and the plain style lucky statuary
23. The design of the private room and the arch are widely divergent from the design of the lobby
24. One corner of the inner area

25. Dim light makes the old-fashioned wooden armchair very awesome.
26. The structure of the gateway is extremely complicated.
27. A huge Buddha is blessing everything right before his eyes.
28. Everything here has a story. The stone tub which looks like a bathtub is actually a mirror.

29. The VIP hall has the most intricate furnishings. Typical factors from Eastern and Western cultures are equally combined
30. The Western fireplace, candlestick and rocking chair go very well with traditional Chinese paintings of beautiful women

31. A corner of a rectangular hall, with bamboo mats fixed to the wall.
32.33. This hall is luxurious as well as private.
34. An armchair with brilliant wood carvings

shanghai tmsk restaurant

Shanghai TMSK Restaurant is located in Xintiandi. It combines both traditional Chinese elements with contemporary coloured glazing design. As soon one enters through the glass door, one is greeted by a coloured glazed screen. From here, the application of coloured glazing pervades throughout the restaurant. The bar, partition screens, walls, barrel vaulted ceiling, floor, tables, lamps and dishware—all show the unique character of coloured glass. The interior lighting is subdued, but the soft, gentle illumination brings the transluscent coloured glass to life, evoking a surreal, dream-like atmosphere. The restaurant has two levels: the focus of the lower level is the bar, while the main dining area is on the upper level. The main design theme reflects is the resplendent of the Tang Dynasty. The bar chairs, with red lantern bases, soften the icy-coloured glass, giving it a rich contemporary atmosphere. The gold foil clad rear wall of the bar, along with a row of glass lamps suspended from the ceiling, enable a clear demarcation of the area. The different kinds of coloured glass that are used throughout the bar make a gorgeous atmosphere. An orchid waterscape, positioned near the stairs which lead to the upper level are a focal point of TMSK. The specific breed of orchid used conveys a relaxing and warm feeling. Another focal point of TMSK is the charming coloured glass hand basin in the washroom. The upper level shows a combination of East-meets-West. Traditional drama and folk music are performed on a mini stage situated on the upper level. The interior of TMSK is really a fairyland of coloured glass.

1. In the lobby of TMSK, the unusual combination of material, pattern and arrangement creates a sense of magnificence
2. The gold-foil-covered wall behind the bar enables a clear hierarchy of the whole area to be read
3. At the simple entry to the restaurant, a glass screen blocks the line of sight
4. The hall
5. Traditional elements serve the purpose of displaying modern interpretations. For example, the dining chairs are reminiscent of the design of curule chairs
6. The blue background wall provides part of the focus of the establishment
7. All the doors and windows are coloured glass, showing the changeable and variable shading
8. The orchid waterscape exhibits the harmonisation of complicated hierarchy and simple background
9. The brick has been carefully chosen. It matches the dining chairs and tables perfectly
10. At one corner of the bar, the simple standing lamp livens the space

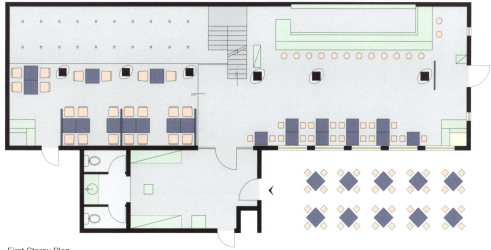

First Storey Plan

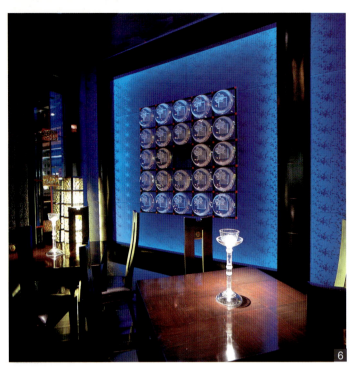

6

7

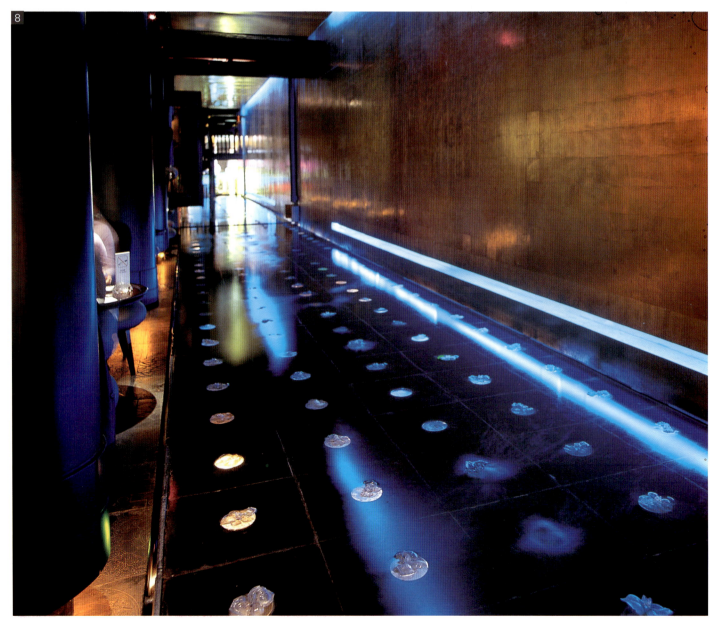

8

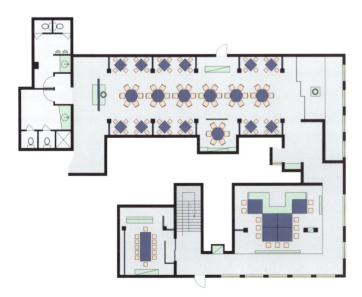

Second Storey Plan

11. The resplendent and elegant lobby is a focal point of the restaurant
12. To help emphasise the character of traditional Chinese culture, a mini stage is included; this is suitable to the performance of traditional drama and folk music
13. A display area for coloured glass
14. The long corridor is interspersed with coloured glass and back-lighting
15. The design of lighting can enrich the visual arrangement
16. A large private room
17. Set against a dark background, the red and yellow lamp light can induce an emotional response
18. Elements projecting traditional Chinese culture: totem pole, brick, lamp and dome
19. The gold foil that is used throughout makes an illustrious environment

level 1 multi-cuisine restaurant

Level 1 Multi-Cuisine Restaurant occupies the first level of the Intercontinental hotel & Resort. It aims to demonstrate an open, modern, vivid and elegant environment. It comprises of coffee bar, sushi area and noodle house. The decorative style - "Zen-conception" welcomes the guests at the entry. Black wooden tables, red velour chairs, brown wooden floor, all of those create the basic theme of the whole restaurant. Set against a lighting background of very rich yellow colour, simple line with luxurious decors and rich material is a contrasting and complementary blend of the noble character. Sushi area is connected with noodle house. Both of them face to a contemporary open kitchen, which is a normal designing style in buffet restaurant. Compared with the closed kitchen, the open kitchen can inspire the customer's appetite, at the same time it needs more strict cooking condition. Close to the open kitchen is the buffet dinning flat. Like other top grade buffet restaurants, the marmoreal table-board matches the wall lamps perfectly. The noodle house is the most traditional Chinese designing style in this restaurant. The design of plain vases and jars enhance the sense of minimalism. "Hang" style calligraphy decorated in the wall and cabinets is the typical oriental symbol.

1. The cloud-shaped lamps help to accentuate the fancy visual effect against the simple, contemporary environment
2. The lobby is characterized by a feel of elegance and modernization
3. The application of lighting promotes the unique character of the whole restaurant
4. The ingenious lamps generate a strong 3-dimensional feeling

5

6

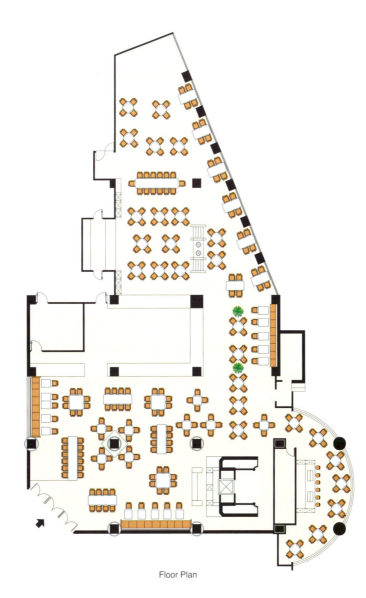

Floor Plan

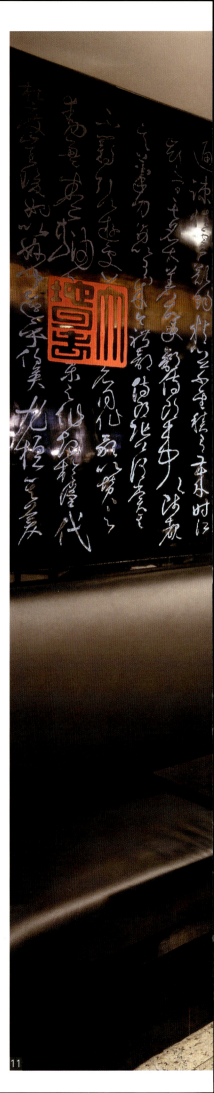

5. A glance at the restaurant
6. The huge column compliments the open space to evoke a spacious environment
7. The clean-lined counter makes no conflict with the column, thus balancing the light and shade effect
8. Well-arranged dining seats in the lobby
9. The glass screen gives a visual sense of layering
10. The unusual combination of calligraphy and cosy dining chairs are unified by the whole atmosphere
11. 180 degree views promote a visually spacious effect
12-13. Full-height glazing widens the vision
14. The buffet counter's simple design meets customers' needs

shark's fin & rice restaurant

Located in the fifth floor of CITIC Square, Shark's Fin & Rice Restaurant has nine private rooms and 100 dining seats. The designer adopted a traditional-meets-contemporary theme in the design of restaurant. He applied a modern Westernized lifestyle, but at the same time remained conscious of Chinese traditional cultural roots. Entering the restaurant, guests will get a feel of silence and elegance. The main style of the restaurant could be described as "simple and fresh,"following the style of the Qing Dynasty. The whole environment has a majestic feeling. Furniture from the Qing dynasty, rosewood dining chairs, wood tea tables, unique palace lanterns and elegant wall decors, are the major focal points of the design. Especially, the inclusion of traditional Qinghua porcelain emphasizes the Oriental cultural sense. All the decoration is not starkly piled up, but well-connected through a blend of past and contemporary elements. A vivid atmosphere is created through the application of carved the wooden sculpture. Fans with different Chinese geometrical patterns serve both the functions of practicalityy and artistic flair. Rosewood panels in vibrant colors with traditional patterns form a partitioned screen. With the main restaurant colour schemed black, yellow and red, prominence is given to the imagery of the traditional Chinese environment.

1. The restaurant is dominated by the application of traditional Chinese furniture and calligraphy
2. "Simple and fresh" is the main design theme of the restaurant. It follows the style of the Qing Dynasty
3. The entry shows a sense of elegance
4. The combination of different cultural elements create a new aesthetic feeling
5. Bamboo curtain cannot be used as a partition, but it serves the function of subtle separation
6. The unusual combination of light-strip and light-spot creates a unitary effect

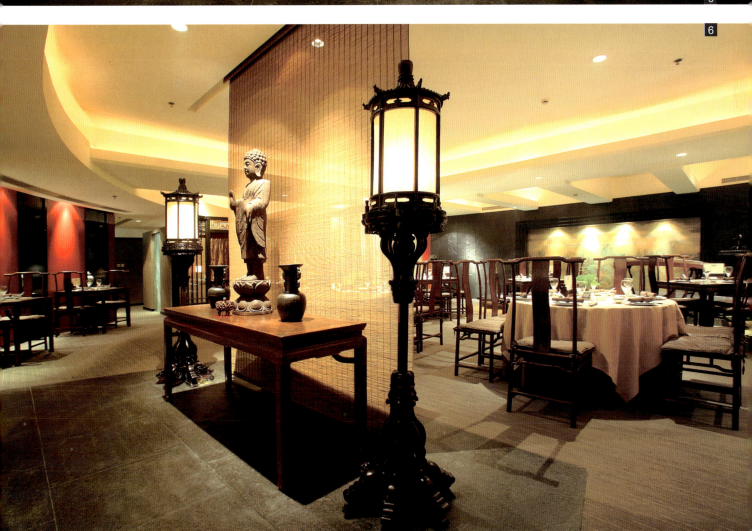

7. A glance at the restaurant
8. The combination of semitransparent valence and red wall promotes the Oriental concept
9. Coupled with soft lighting, the valence appears as a visual contrast with its environment
10. Coupled with brown-coloured blocks, the whole environment achieves a magestic feeling
11. The dining seats and dishware exhibit the harmonization of East-meets-West
12. Without heavy decoration, the top structure also projects an elegant feeling
13. Partial connection to the outside world promptsthe feeling of a visually spacious area
14. The application of square and round elements enriches the details of the design

15. A glance at the private room
16. The form of the chairs and tables do not represent something old and dreary, but something new and refined
17. The combination of red and green coloured blocks are a unique design point
18. Simple partitions with golden flower carvings bring forth a typical Chinese atmosphere
19. The lighting makes for an elegant atmosphere
20. The entry of the restaurant
21. Mysterious and silent corridor
22. An arch-shaped door and a rock garden hint at a typical Oriental culture
23. Beautifully coloured blocks are a major feature of the restaurant
24. The door, wall, lighting and antique statuary, all help to complete the visual structure
25. Even the view of the corridor is well designed

soahc restaurant & tea garden

Similar to most elegant old buildings in Shanghai, the Soahc Restaurant & Tea Garden, located in the south lane of Xintiandi combines beautiful contemporary style with old traditional Shikume style. Based on this particular eastern style, the whole teahouse adopts an East-meets-West theme, specially conceived by its host. The entrance leads to a lobby in which a floating platform atop an irregularly shaped pool sees the original airwell converted into a simplified Oriental courtyard. The water cascades down from the pilaster on the second floor, the color matching the carp in the pool perfectly. The Dining Room is decorated with luxuriant colors to reveal its character of elegance and grandeur. The overall character of this area is proclaimed through the colorful dining chairs and splendid porcelain dish-ware. The elegant Western-style is fully absorbed into the design, through, for example, luxuriant European wall lamps, Tiffany antique porcelain vase and large murals. The most dazzling elements are the screens and the optical fibre. These decorations enrich the whole environment. What's more, the Chinese style windows displace our sense of space and time.

1. The building is over 80 years old
2. Soahc Restaurant and Tea Garden lies within the original 2-storey structure
3. Colourful glass in specific motifs separate the whole space into its many various parts
4. A ventilated, but not exposed, private space is naturally separated by a thick bamboo curtain
5. The feint pattern on the ceiling mimics the shadows cast by the wall lamps
6. A cascade of water flows down continuously, leading the way to the pool

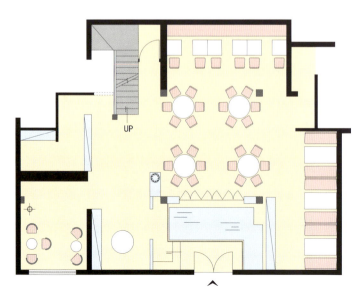

First Storey Plan

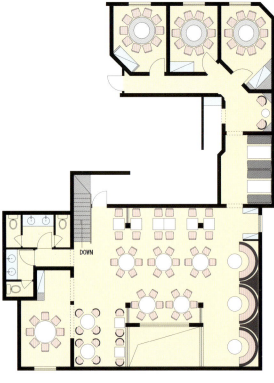
Second Storey Plan

7. With its various colours, the inner space presents an elegant and splendid style combining both Eastern and Western characteristics
8. Classic and modern shapes are well blended
9. Dining tables
10. The colourful chairs and porcelain dish-ware all illustrate the unique character of the teahouse
11. A glance at the Soahc Restaurant and Tea Garden

12. The sub-dining area (separated from the main area) emphasizes the Oriental theme by using silk Chinese lamps with a modern style
13. The sense of relaxation pervades throughout the teahouse, which perfectly responds to the business idea
14. Though the space of adjacent dining areas is limited, the high ceiling dome and the clever use of lighting produce a visually spacious effect
15. The heavy and complicated pave, the . style dining table and the Tiffany antiques create a strong visual impact
16. A large wall mural prompts a peaceful feeling
17. The logo of the teahouse acts as an attractive decorative element in the space
18. This narrow space accommodates just two dining tables. Elaborated design with large appliquéretains coherence with the surrounding style
19. The foyer area has its own character. The curved red leather chairs suit the windows and the abstract graphics very well.
20. A view of the corridor on the second floor
21. The cellaret and the stair balustrade create an elaborate view

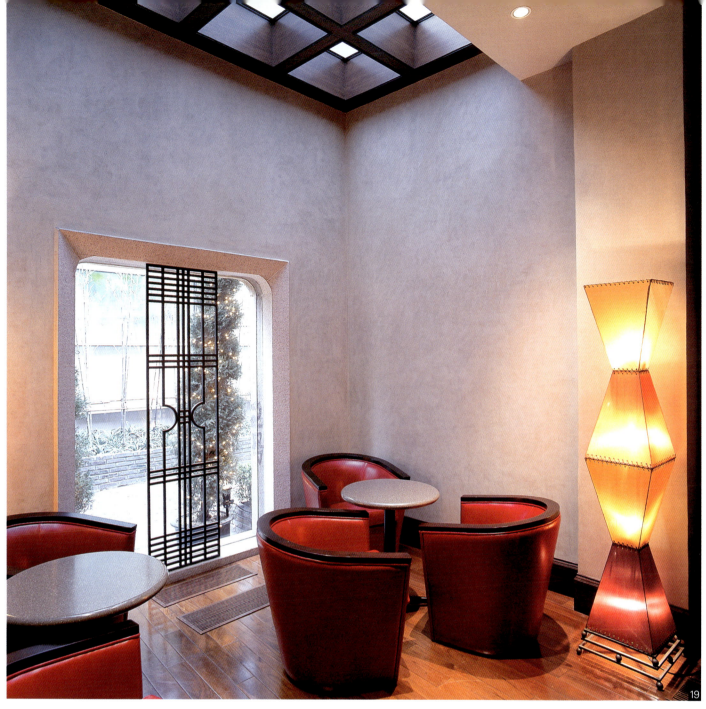

shintori null II

Located at the Julu Road, Shintori Null II is a Japanese Restaurant specializing in Kaiseki food. Infusing Eastern and Western tastes, its entire design style corresponds both to Zen theory ("nature", "plain" and "elegance") and also the simplicity of the last century. A flourishing world appears after one enters the concrete corridor filled with bamboo. Simplicity reigns in the dining room, which was restructured from a cinema measuring 27m in length, 20m in width and 10m in height, a central open area and private rooms at two sides are kept in their original style. Without unnecessary decorations, the bare steel structure, transparent glass and rough concrete make a strong visual impact. Views of the open-kitchen at the first floor can be seen from the either side of the seating area. The use of inclined mirror and full-height glazing brightens the space. The courtyard is decorated with Oriental style "Dry Landscape", paved with white gravel. The geometric aesthetic is directly and strongly expressed in the design, creating a successful space.

1. The logo is presented in a subtle way
2. Simplicity also reigns on the second floor
3. MenZhong bamboo is a special symbol of SHINTORI NULL II
4. Pots placed at the entrance are used as containers for rain gear

5. Broken bricks make a strong visual impact against the colour of the interior
6. The most direct means were used to express the geometric aesthetic feeling
7. Circulation space, with no indication of what is hidden in the thick bamboo
8. The voidal space of the mirror endows both clarity and uncertainty
9. Escaping from the noisy city, the guests can enjoy themselves in the easy atmosphere here
10. Downlighting plays an important role
11. The low level in the middle of the restaurant is sunken like a valley

12. The steel structure emphasizes a sense of power
13. The original structure of a cinema has been kept, making the space feel very large
14. Overlooking the open kitchen
15. In the open kitchen, the whole process of cooking can be observed, thus diminishing the gap between the guests and the restaurant

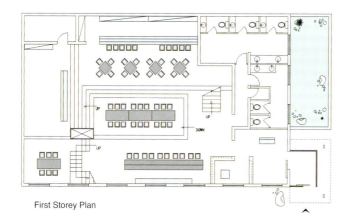

First Storey Plan

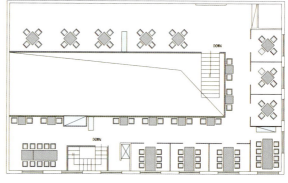

Second Storey Plan

16. Besides providing light, large windows provide better outdoor views
17. The dishware and material on the table for sushi making are all elaborately selected
18. Well-arranged bar
19. The arrangement of the seats is entirely according to the designer's preference
20. More views are reflected from this specially positioned mirror
21. These extravagant Western-style seats were specifically selected for their height, and perfectly match this large room
22. Repetitive use of lines and planes has unified various isolated elements under a minimalist style
23. Glass, wood and stones are evident in the corridor, showing a natural and simple "Zen" design sense
24. A self-produced vessel is used for decoration
25. The courtyard is decorated with an Oriental style "dry landscape". The yard outside the lavatory has also been designed in detail

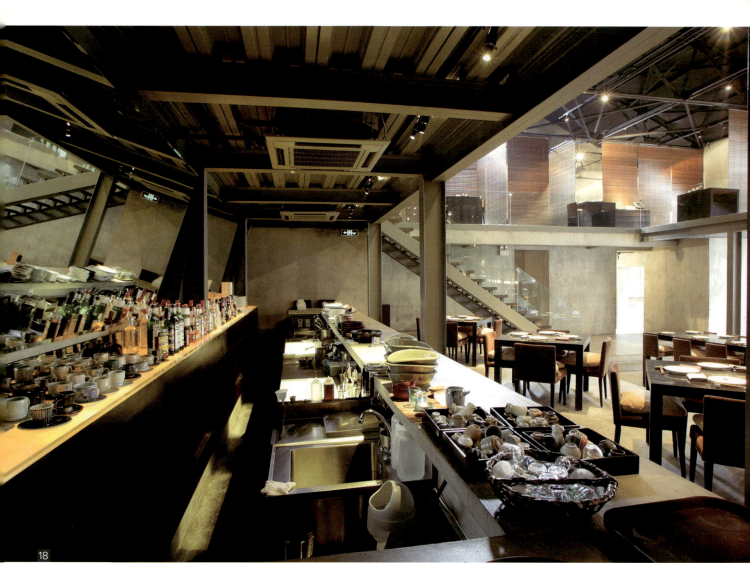

18

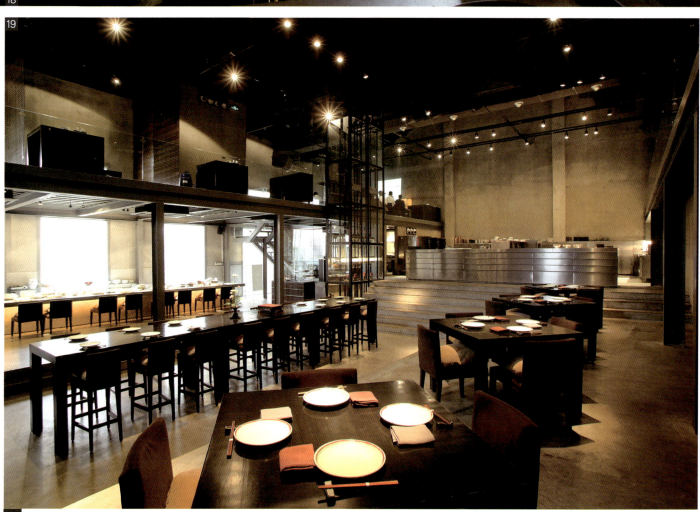

19

zen
zen

A white wall with a slick curve and lotus flower-style lights greet guests, thus showing a mysterious, solemn, but smooth and lovely atmosphere. The English designer of Zen adopted a mixture of both modernistic and the *Shikumen* characters. He felt that the nostalgic culture should be elaborated on. Hence, he retained the *Shikumen* facade. From the main interior color black, it was easier to extrude the essence of Shikumen. A pond at the entry shows the concise nature of a European garden. A circular skylight and round-edged chairs and tables project a vivid feel. The designer also made a cocoon-style partition between the restaurant and kitchen, thus increasing the thickness of the inner wall. Space, lighting, music, view and the multi-culture - all of these have great impact on the design concept of the restaurant. The Zen-conception directs the main idea of this restaurant, for which a modern design technique and light-shadow have created a unique space. This traditional building infuses ancient elements to contemporary design character. The wavy white interior wall is just like a continuous white cocoon and the glass windows within it seem to break its flow. The lotus flower-light is just like retro-Buddhism. It has a unique quality of light and shadow, using a unique blend of Chinese Buddhism and advanced expression.

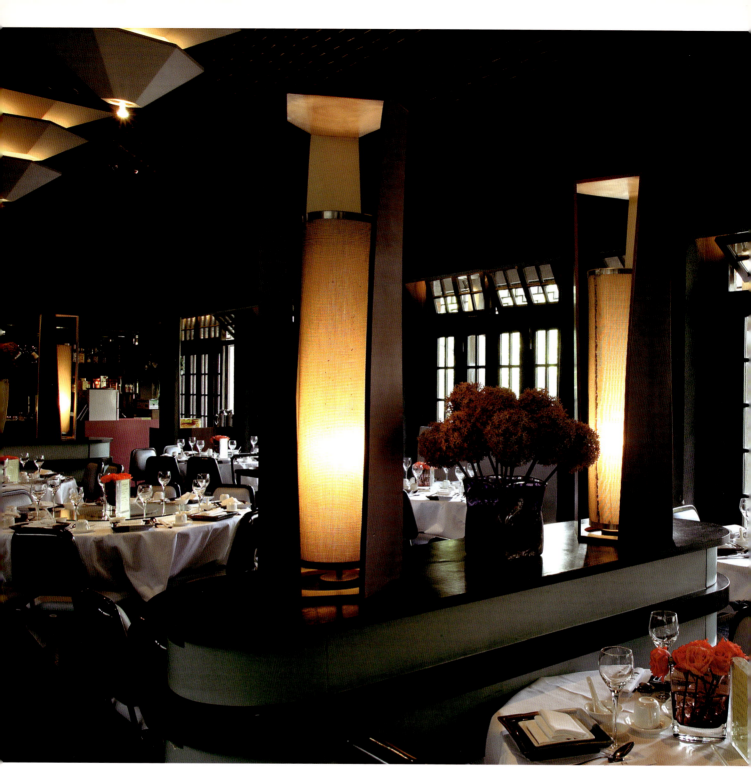

1. The exterior of Zen. It was the first building in XinTianDi, and sits opposite the "former address of First Conference of Communist Party"
2. The arrangement of seats is comfortable
3. The panorama of Zen's lobby
4. Separation of different zones
5. Subdued lighting is important for the special lighting design
6. The curved wall shows a perfect blend of innovation and vividness, eschewing white-wall monotony

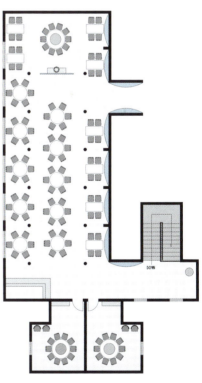

2nd Storey plan

1st Storey plan

12

7. Lighting in the inner dining area of the lobby makes a comfortable and cosy environment
8. The geometrically-styled lotus light creates a unique light-shadow effect with a unique blend of Chinese Buddhism and advanced expression
9. A bar attached to the restaurant; the full-height window follows the original Shikumen style
10. A cocoon style partition is made between the restaurant and kitchen. The message is that the cocoon will take a long time to become a butterfly, which is just the same process as the food in the kitchen
11. The stairs of the entry show the simple modern style, however, the rounded pool also emphasizes the Eastern Zen conception
12. The modernistic atmosphere of the Private Room
13. One corner of the restaurant; all tables and chairs are round-edged

park 97

Sensationally contrasting pieces come together in a harmonious match. Baci is another restaurant which shows a unique Italian style, but also takes on the character of Japanese dinning areas—comfortable, contemporary and relaxing. A visually spacious environment is created with a mirror-clad ceiling. This area is dominated by touches of uncluttered simplicity with a monochromatic color scheme. The combination of white dining table cloths and the dark dining chairs creates a striking visual effect. Irregular alternate arrangement of wooden floor board and marble flooring also separates the corridor and dining area. Chinese-style columns with concealed lighting and stripe glass not only evoke a special visual effect, but also soften the environment. In the cosy sofa foyer area, the wooden lover-seat and the alluring wall pictures contribute to the creative design of this restaurant.

1. The witty play of a stepping wall allows elegant views of FuXing Park
2. The red brick wall adds to the romantic French character of FuXing Park
3. The dining chair upholstery creates a striking visual effect

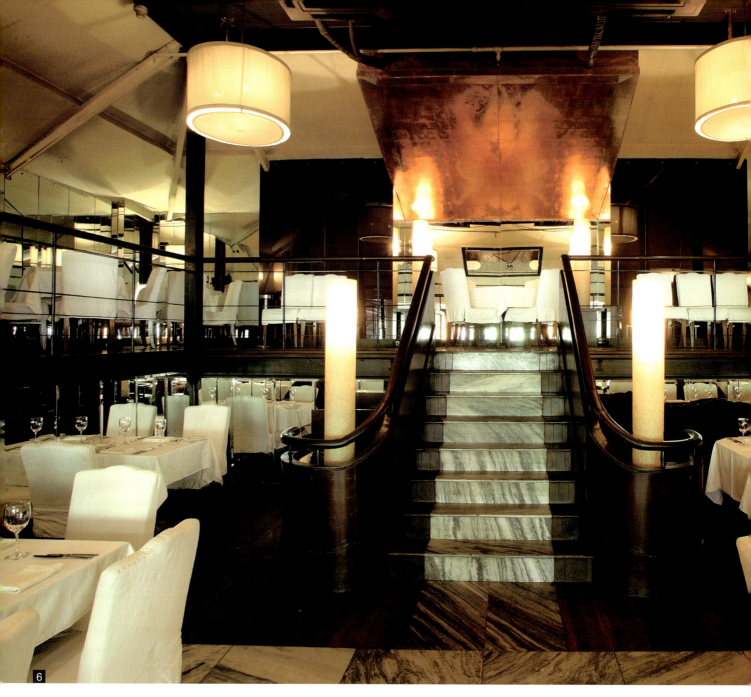

4. White dining seats evoke a fresh and comfortable atmosphere
5. Wall lamps adopt the same style of the Japanese dining area, thus enhancing the sense of minimalism
6. A visually spacious environment is created with the mirror-clad ceiling. This area is dominated by touches of uncluttered simplicity with a monochromatic colour scheme
7. The elegant dining area is arranged symmetrically
8. The tailor-made translucent beige shoji lamp provides an artistic feeling as well as sufficient lighting

9. Simple layered mirror on the ceiling enriches the environment of the restaurant
10. The spacious dining area follows the original structure and offers more comfortable dining seats
11. A glance at the restaurant
12. The simple and cosy dining area is in the typical design style of an Italian restaurant
13. A large mirror enables the second floor to appear visually spacious
14. The arrangement of separating the dining area is successful. Suitable distances afford the spaces a semi-private feel

15. The seductive wall mural adds a touch of brightness to the whole restaurant
16. The focus in this area falls to the red flowers, which are illuminated brightly
17. Set against a background of shining metal and light, the white dining seats convey a relaxing and warm feeling
18. The irregular geometric forms cutting into the mural ventilate the dining areas, and also evoke a modern and relaxing atmosphere

19. The concealed light fittings in the columns create a special effect
20. A glance at Tokio Joe
21. A sensational contrast achieves a harmonious match
22. The private room of Tokio Joe

san qian yuan sqy

Located on Wulumuqi Road, close to Hengshan Road, San Qian Yuan SQY is a multi-functional restaurant (including bar). The whole construction is like two rectangles piled up. The upper one is a glass rectangle and the exposed girders and columns of the one below recall a Japanese sensibility. The combination of glass and wooden structure evokes a modern feeling. The wooden floor comes from an Old Shanghai warehouse. The wine shelf is screw thread style. The elegant wine bottles make a wonderful contrast with the tough wine shelf. The arrangement of the second floor is compact and is well ventilated. All sides are glazed, thus infusing the space into the exterior environment. The main design concept is the Old Shanghai construction style. It becomes an enjoyment to look at the outside world from within, especially since there is an English country villa behind Sanqianyuan. The designer adopted a mix technique for both interior and exterior; for example, totally different materials compose the columns of the first floor. The blend of furnishing elements from the Chinese and Japanese cultures is both contrasting and complimentary.

1. The calligraphy of the restaurant
2. Transparent full-height windows and ceiling work together to create a cosy atmosphere
3. A glance at the restaurant
4. The vestibule of San Qian Yuan serves the function of afternoon tea site
5. The buffet dining counter
6. The gate of the restaurant

First Storey Plan

7. The whole construction is like two rectangles piled up. The upper one is glass. The exposed girders and columns of the one below recall a Japanese sensibility
8. The fountain completes the contemporary feel of the whole restaurant
9. Simplicity is the main design theme of the restaurant. Steel structure, glass walls and wooden floors all give a sense of layering
10. The combination of glass and wood evokes a modern feeling

11. The use of local materials was a major design concept. All of them came from Shanghai
12. The arrangement of dining seats is based on the terrace style
13. One corner of the restaurant
14. The second floor of the bar

15. Touches of rusticity pepper the space
16. The spacious design style refers back to the designer's original concept
17. A glance at the second floor

18

19

20

18. The density of the calligraphy shows a striking contrast to the glass
19. Both the old decorative elements and the wood help to accentuate the historic feeling of the restaurant
20. The Japanese room on the first floor projects a Japanese architectural style
21. The main design theme of the first floor is simple and "Zen" in style
22. The exquisite designing style of the dining area shows the typical style of the restaurant
23. The whole space is filled with a feel of truth and nature through the application of timber
24. The first level bar
25. The design of the Western-style bar goes well with the whole restaurant

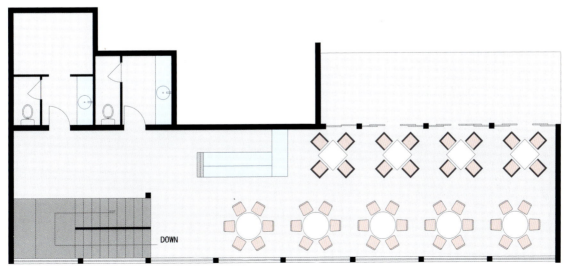

Second Storey Plan

banker cafe

Situated within Hong Kong Plaza, which is located in a bustling shopping area in Shanghai, Banker Cafe serves normal fast food similar to those found in traditional Hong Kong cafes. Combining contemporary business concepts and traditional elements of Chinese design, Banker Cafe is a perfect blend of the Eastern culture in a contemporary design setting. The entrance to the Banker Cafe projects a strong Oriental feel. Simple line drawings of Chinese Gods are set against a red background, offering a fresh perspective to way the Gods are traditionally drawn and perceived. According the architectural principles of the Zhou Dynasty, color is the most important element in the expression of hierarchy and style. The designer of Banker Cafe, however, did away with the way color is traditionally employed in interior design, and thus, combined the bold symbolic colors of the East with a contemporary reds from the Western palette. Multi-colored table cloths add to the lively ambience of the space, while the gridded ceiling unifies the different elements on the ceiling.

1. The symbolic signage outside the Banker Caf* is the best advertisement for the restaurant
2. Multicoloured dining tables are intended to induce appetite. The space has a simple and fresh atmosphere
3. Practicability is the main design theme. The contemporary designing style replaces the traditional ceremonious element
4. Coupled with the animal ring, the exaggerated and contemporary design of the door combines traditional eastern structural design with the new aestheticism
5. The miniscape of white sandstone and vegetation in the corner inspires the customer to imagine a continental scene
6. Imagery of the guard spirit clads a decorative wall, whose colour matches the space perfectly

7. Potted plants bring nature back into the urban environment
8. Booth seating is typical in the café

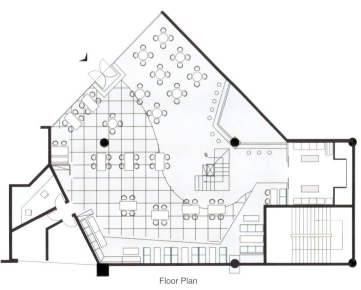

Floor Plan

9. The space has no splendid traditional decorations. Yet the gridded ceiling manages to unite all the diverse details inan encompassing manner
10. The blue background panel balances well with the vivid personality of the rest of the café. Science fiction d*cor prompts the imagination
11. On the glass entry door, the guardian spirit, set on a red background, offers a fresh perspective of East-meets-West

shanghai uncle restaurant

Shanghai Uncle Restaurant is located on the eighth floor of Times Square in PuDong district. A contemporary design concept pervades throughout the whole restaurant. The idea was to create a modern, Western-influenced interior space, but at the same time, the design had to reflect the cultural roots of the Chinese. Combining traditional Chinese cuisine with advanced cooking techniques, Shanghai Uncle Restaurant showcases a blending of gastronomic fares from the East and West. The national flower, the peony, is used repetively throughout the interior, even on the motifs of cushion covers and table cloths. The peony represents wealth and prosperity, and is an important symbol in the Chinese culture. High-backed chairs, inclined at a slight angle and adorned with peony motifs, project Western luxury and extravagance, while maintaining the intricasies of the Chinese culture. The spatial layout of the restaurant is planned such that moving through the space becomes an imaginary experience through a "Chinese landscape painting." Although not strictly planned according to its formalistic principles, it, however, adopts elements like the suspended corridor and sweeping staircase to give the feeling of suspension and dynamic movement throughout the space.

1. With Chinese architectural art in mind, the designer paid much attention to the spatial arrangement
2. The carved dragon-shaped light fittings convey an elegant and luxuriant feeling, even though the designer has simplified much of the other traditional decoration
3. Hanging above the atrium is a large, elegant red lamp with a diameter of 2 metres.
4. The focus of the restaurant falls to the national flower - the peony. The peony is said to bring wealth and propitiousness
5. The angular-shaped restaurant projects a comfortable open dining atmosphere
6. The Chinese red valence is unique and brilliantly toned
7. The design of the double volume space is modelled on the "fairytale" interiors of the Qing Dynasty, giving the space a degree of delicacy and elegance
8. The cabbage pal perfects the free style of the whole environment

9. The whole space retains the feel of a Oriental pavilion
10. Full-height windows soften the visual effect
11. A transition of upstairs and downstairs spaces

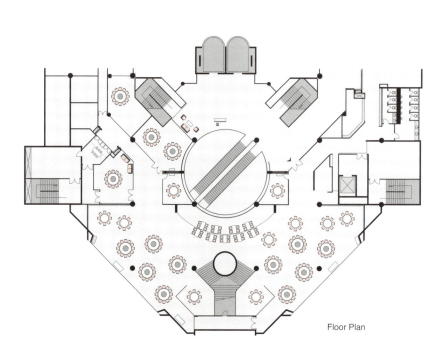

Floor Plan

12. A movable door separates the peony-shaped room
13. Crystal curtains and transparent glass enhance the sense of the contemporary
14. Different colour blocks evoke a vivid atmosphere
15. Set against a background of wall pictures is a complenentary blend of furnishing elements from the East and the West
16. An irregularly patterned carpet brings a vivid feel
17. The rest of the restaurant serves both its practical function and enriches the overall effect with luxury and comfort
18. The imaginative canvasses create a magnificent artistic atmosphere
19. This room can accommodate all kinds of large-scale activities
20. The elegant entry to the restaurant
21. The wine cabinet draws attention

liu hui guan restaurant

Located in the south lane of Xintiandi, Liu Hui Guan Restaurant specializes in Sichuan cuisine and crab dishes. Upon entering the restaurant, one will feel a sense of calm and serenity. The main business area occupies the second floor facing the commercial district along the main road. Light and dark shades of timber fill the lobby area, giving it an air of understated elegance. Four private rooms—aptly named "Spring", "Summer", "Autumn" and "Winter"— reflect the quaint character of the restaurant. A witty protrayal of two Gods of Marriage standing by the screen at the entrance, with blades made of corn, sets the mood for the gastronomic event to come. A stone doorframe is used at the main entrance gate. Comparing this with the ones commonly seen in traditional houses, the design of the main entrance, with the insertion of glass doors for practical purposes, sensitively incorporates modern amenities in a historical building. The design of the restaurant retains the old constructional techniques of Shanghai, right down to the details on the door and motifs on the balcony. The overall design, reflective of typical Shanghainese architecture and design, captures the essence of Shanghai's historical past. Liu Hui Guan's expanding business has led to the creation of a new annex that is high-tech and contemporary, distinctly different in feel from its adjoining, more traditional dining area.

1. The spacious lobby
2. Liu Hui Guan is infused into the old construction perfectly
3. A three-dimensional picture wall brings out a strong country atmosphere
4. The surface articulation of the modern column surface reflects the traditional method of construction
5. The windows project a classic elegant feel
6. The valence partition creates another zone
7. Services are left exposed on the ceiling. This brings a unique modern twist

8. The classic Chinese dining chairs give the restaurant a feel of simplicity and elegance
9. The pendant lamp makes a striking image
10. The dining chairs are arranged in an uncommon fashion - two either side of a round table. Yet, the arrangement is comfortable and cosy
11. A different language of lines and planes is employed in the private room
12. The arrangement of the dining tables adopts an East-meets-West philosophy

13. The design of the upstairs vestibule is quite cosy, facilitating a good view across to the other lane
14. A glance at the restaurant
15. A perfect blend of contemporary style and traditional arrangement
16. A relaxed atmosphere is achieved as light filters in through translucent glass
17. Although a calm air permeates, there are also vivid instances in the design
18. A transparent ceiling breaks the silence of tiles
19. Blue-grey tiles with a delicate design mark a transition space

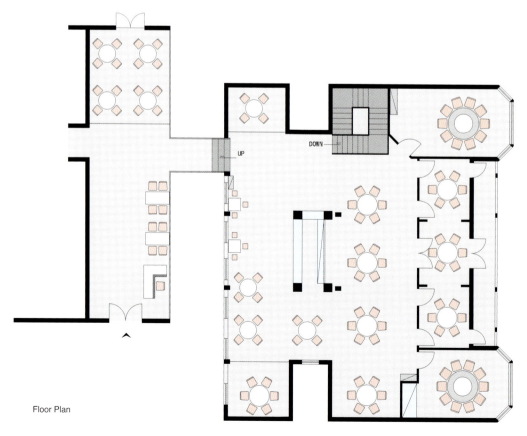

Floor Plan

lipis lazuli international

Lipis Lazuli exudes a strong cultural influence of the Jiangnan Province. Its timber structure and staircase, natural stone walls, and wall murals are reminiscent of a traiditonal home in an old town. The space of the restaurant is relatively small and narrow. However, the tables are laid-out in a linear fashion, making the space bigger appear than it really is. The subdued lighting in the interior gives an illusion of spatial continuity, sublty stretching the eye to the exterior of the restaurant, dimly lit by street lamps. The decor is a fusion of the East and West, employing Western cultural influences, like the long dining table, and set against a more ornamented Oriental dining chairs.

1. A corner of the lobby
2. The mixture of timber steps on the gateway and glass makes a distinctive contrast

3. The arrangement of a long dining table and armchairs is actually very modern
4. The tableware is Western: knives and forks. But the suit the atmosphere very well

5. In a limited space, the dining tables and chairs are well arranged so that the space seems larger
6. Sheepskin pumpkin lanterns hanging from the ceiling are a good match for the coarse stone walls
7. A bird cage makes a quaint ornament

mei long zhen restaurant

Everyone who visits Mei Long Zhen restaurant will be attracted by its traditional Chinese style immediately—the decorated archway, the delicate wood carvings, the Ming Dynasty-style mahogany furniture, the calligraphy and paintings by famous artists and personalities, as well as quaint banquet halls.

Mei Long Zhen Restaurant, with a floor area of 2,500 square meters was first established in 1938. It has 24 distinguished guests halls, as well as numerous halls which hold 2, 3 or 6 tables each.

en restaurant

4

1. Gateway of Mei Long Zhen Restaurant
2. The Phoenix Hall
3. A magnificent distinguished guests hall in a Chinese palace style
4. The Phoenix Hall
5. View of distinguished guests hall
6-9. The interior is lavished with richly coloured timbers

10-11. Magnificent hall. The well placed three-dimensional wood carvings on the ceiling stir the imagination. One side wall is designed as an imitation of an antique gallery, while a mirror occupies the opposite wall. It reflects the scenography in the hall and the light from palace lanterns, therefore broadening the visual field

12-13. Timber is the main material used in the halls. The delicate nature of the interior decoration brings a hint of the luxurious ancient palace lifestyle to the present

14-19. Glass and glass paintings make the small halls seem much more spacious

20-21 Decorated relief ceilings and palace lanterns make these halls beautiful and imposing
22-23 A play of differently toned timbers brings vibrancy to these heavily timbered halls.

si fang cai restaurant

As one enters the Si Fang Cai Restaurant through the passage bordered by a little pair of humble timber doors, one encounters a roomy and well-lit interior space that was once the residence of a wealthy family. The restaurant, situated in a traditional residential area, is divided into two main levels—a lower dining area, and a relatively more private upper level. Tables are well spaced apart, there's an overwhelming sense of spaciousness and homeliness. The space is an ingenious application of the rustic and the modern, especially achieved through the expression and articulation of materials. Rustic materials such as brick and twine are persuaded to take up innovative forms and one may even see the surprising insertion of industrial fittings. In salient areas, the restaurant may appear to be fully conservative, using only traditional furniture and lighting elements, but these areas metamorphosize to utimately creating a restaurant which is at once old and new.

1. A simple gateway of naturally finished timber marks the entrance
2. Woodwork and finely-woven rope are combined in a rustic manner, bringing the restaurant a folk ambience
3. A warm yellow paint is set against the darker timber furniture
4. A mezzanine level maximises the limited space, also promoting a new spatial conception

5. Rustic brickwork is used in a gentle manner, creating a curved counter. The red tones of the bricks are picked up by the floor tiles and the decorative elements in the kitchen
6. Classical Chinese elements pepper the rustic interior. A delicately proportioned standing lamp makes a strong, yet subtle, juxtaposition with the heavy outline of a timber window frame
7. Glimpses to the adjacent space are layered by a woven screen element
8. The surface articulation of the brickwork is sensitive to the articulations on traditional Chinese screen elements
9-10. A varied and interesting combination of timber elements in an ox horn shape, and coarse fibrous rope, replace the common flat ceiling. This is an attempt by the designer to showcase ideas inspired by the new artistic ideology of the West.
11-13. Furniture is simply shaped and positioned in the space with clarity.

hei san yu zhuang

This is a Sichuan food restaurant in Shanghai. Uniquely different from the surrounding buildings, the facade of the restaurant looks like a wine shop in a fishing village, bringing forth an ocean atmosphere. The signs and couplets on the interior walls also enhance the joyous moods.

3

1. The unique facade of the restaurant
2. Exterior wall finishes are reflected in the interior
3. There is an emphasis on decorating the interior, rather than carrying out extensive built work Segments of raw textile hang from the ceiling, depicting a form of "simplicity"– perhaps small ripples on the ocean surface
4. Rough wall plaster contrasts with the smooth textile segments

5. Heavy, rustic timber beams and columns are suggestive of the "folk lifestyle" that one would experience in a fishing village
6. Other timber elements echo the style

7. The "homestyle" feel of the restaurant is reinforced by the eclectic ceramicware
8. Simple low stools casually accompany the heavily grained timber tables
9. Note the ingenious use of earthen urns as light fittings
10. The ceiling too is roughly plastered
11. The feel of the establishment may be casual, but careful placement of items avoids a chaotic interior

a-money restaurant

The designer adopted a classic-meets-contemporary theme in the design of A-Money Restaurant. The main color scheme of the restaurant is black. Huge frameless windows allow the space to be filled with natural light. Being transverse in nature, the spatial and visual layout play up the superimposition of both horizontal and vertical elements. A composition of steel frames and glass screens give the high-ceiling space rhythm and visual interest, while visually separating the space into several areas. The combination of black and grey marble table-board and white flooring give a classic yet trendy feel to the restaurant. At the same time, gold and red walls break the black-white monotones, giving it points of visual focus and highlight. A clever play of straw adds texture to the space as well as accentuates the rich golden color of the walls.

1. The combination of stainless steel and glass is perfect for the style of the restaurant
2. A glance at the restaurant
3. The focus of the restaurant is the visual spaciousness
4. Several private rooms meet the commercial need of the HongQiao area
5. A backlit "lightwell" creates a unique decorative effect

6. The suspended beams suit the environment well
7. Full-height windows make a bridge between the interior and exterior
8. Square and round dining tables meet practical needs
9. The seating arrangement is quite cosy and comfortable. It also infases the traditional Oriental elements

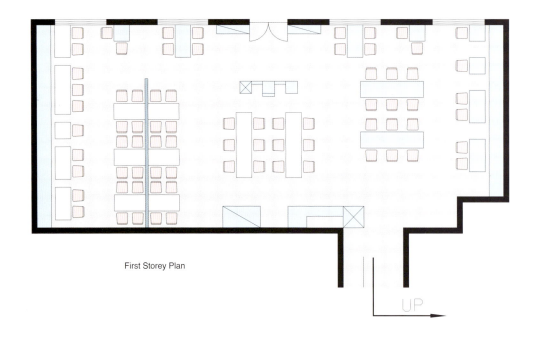

First Storey Plan

10. The mysterious logo of A-Monet Restaurant is the best ornament
11. Sandblasted glass blends the Oriental and Western cultural elements
12. The background decoration enriches the simplicity of the whole environment
13. Lighting and colour add vividness

xintiandi shanghai

Xintiandi Shanghai, a mixed structure with a four-story main building, was built in the early 20th century. This historical building was formerly occupied by a stationary shop, a school, was the residence of Mao Boyang, was a machinery department and a company's quarters. Its beautiful architecture and rich history, made it a perfect venue for Xintiandi Shanghai when it occupied the building in 2001. In order to retain the old world charm of the place, the designers of Xintiandi Shanghai went through an elaborate process of restoration to preserve the architectural merits of the building. Keeping modern intervention to a minimal, the spirit and essence of the building are meticulously kept by following strict conservation guidelines and details. The designers of this exclusive restaurant borrowed elements from the past, gave them a twist of modernity and sensitively incorporated them into the design of the building. Mostly used as a venue for private events, the space speaks of exclusivity, class and fine dining. Dark wood is used against pale cream walls and decorative fabrics to evoke nostalgia, a memory of Shanghai's European influence on its cultural heritage.

1. Interior decoration remains old in style
2. The exterior
3. The interior decoration is restricted in order to provide a harmonious atmosphere for the furnishings and structure
4. The original door of the structure is a feature in interior decoration. The designer skillfully dealt with the relationship between the furnishings and the original doors

5-8. Dark furniture on a dark timber floor is highlighted beautifully against a warm golden wall colour

9-11. The charming features and nooks of a home enliven the space

12-13. The most significant feature is the roof. The original timber structure and lining effectively communicate the age of the building

index

a-money restaurant
No. 1482, Hongqiao Lu, Shanghai
Postal code: 200336
Tel: 021-6209 7929

banker cafe
S128, F1, Hong Kong Square South Building, No. 283, Huaihai Zhonglu, Shanghai
Postal code: 200020
Tel: 021-6390 6877

crystal jade restaurant
2f-12a-b, 6-7, Xintiandi Square Nanli, 123 Lane, Xingye Lu, Shanghai
Postal code: 200021
Tel: 021-6385 8752

hei san yu zhuang
3-102, Meishi Street, Wanke
City Garden, Shanghai
Postal code: 201101
Tel: 021-6419 3447

level 1 multi-cuisine restaurant
F1, Hotel Inter-continental Pudong Shanghai, No. 777, Zhangyang Lu, Pudong New District, Shanghai
Postal code: 200120
Tel: 021-5831 8888

liu hui guan restaurant
2F, No. 338, Zizhong Lu, Shanghai
Postal code: 200021
Tel: 021-6385 0188

lipis lazuli international
No. 9, Dongping Lu, Shanghai
Postal code: 200031
Tel: 021-6473 1021

index

mei long zhen restaurant
1081, Nanjing Xilu, Shanghai
Postal code: 200041
Tel: 021-6256 6688

park 97
2-A, Gaolan Lu, Shanghai
Postal code: 200020
Tel: 021-5383 2088

people 6
150, Yueyang Road, Xuhui District, Shanghai
Postal code: 200031
Tel: 021-6466 0505

san qian yuan sqy
No. 64, Wulumuqi Nanlu, Shanghai
Postal code: 200031
Tel: 021-6474 3000

shanghai tmsk restaurant
11-2, Xintiandi Square Beili, Lane 181, Taicang Road, Shanghai
Postal code: 200021
Tel: 021-6326 2227

shanghai uncle restaurant
8F, Pudong Times Squre, No. 500, Zhangyang Lu, Shanghai
Postal code: 200120
Tel: 021-5836 7977

shark's fin & rice restaurant
F2, Wanhao Hongqiao Hotel, No.2270, Hongqiao Lu, Shanghai
Postal code: 200336
Tel: 021-6237 6977

index

soahc restaurant & tea garden
No. 3, Xintiandi Square Nanli, Lane 123, Xingye Lu, Shanghai
Postal code: 200021
Tel: 021-6385 7777

si fang cai restaurant
115-B, Changshu Lu, Shanghai
Tel: 021-5403 0405

shintori null II
No. 803, Julu Lu, Jing'an District, Shanghai
Postal code: 200040
Tel: 021-5404 5252

the door restaurant & bar
No. 1468, Hongqiao Lu, Shanghai
Postal code: 200336
Tel: 021-6295 3737

xintiandi shanghai
No. 1, Xintiandi Square Beili, Lane 181, Taicang Lu, Shanghai
Postal code: 200021
Tel: 021-6419 3447

yè shanghai
Xintiandi Square, 338, Huangpo Nanlu, Shanghai
Postal code: 200021
Tel: 021-6331 2323

zen
No. 2, Xintiandi Square Nanli, Lane 123, Xingye Lu, Shanghai
Postal Code: 200021
Tel: 021-6385 6385